THE WORLD PRESS PRESENTS

LEADING
IN THE MIDST OF
FOLLOWERS

THE SECRETS
OF GREAT
LEADERS

J. Konrad Hölè

Proverbs 4:7 says, "Wisdom is the Principle
thing." Wisdom is the only proof that you are
being **"Mentored"** by the **"Most Intelligent
Person In The Universe,"** the **"Holy Spirit."**

Unless otherwise indicated, all Scripture quotations are taken from the King James Version of the Bible.

Leading in the Midst of Followers

Copyright © 1996 by J. Konrad Höle
ISBN 1-888696-06-0
Spirit & Life Ministries
P.O. Box 41010
Minneapolis, MN 55441

Published by
The World Press
P.O. Box 41010
Minneapolis, MN 55441

FORWARD

My Grandmother Bradway who was a pioneer of the Pentecostal movement on the east coast along with my grandfather, would always tell me when discussing peoples involvement in their ministry, and eventually in my ministry, "Cream always rises to the top." I have held on to that statement over the last several years of ministry service, and from that have come to see by experience, and by observation, the vast differences that set great leaders aside from average ones.

I am a person I'm sure much like you, who gets tired at times by listening to the same cliché phrases and words, that one can become accustom to in the church world, or even in secular society and I reach a point where I demand to know how success of God's word, and the blessings of His covenant with us, can work.

There are reasons people succeed, there are reasons people fail, and I have attempted in this book to share with you some of my observations on the reason why great leaders fly like eagles, and average leaders waddle like ducks.

Always remember there is a leader in you, and you are always the link to somebody else's breakthrough, and you will always be led by the Holy Spirit to people who will see you as a bridge to their future.

Be God's leader.

Much love.

J. Konrad Hölè

DEDICATION

I have had the privilege of being radically affected by great leaders in my life, and the misfortune of being tragically affected by bad leaders in my life.

However I am only where I am at today in the work of God, because God has given me the privilege of learning from some of His choicest leaders in this generation.

This book is dedicated to every pastor who has given his/her life to lead God's people effectively out of their Egypt, and into their Promised Land.

To every single mom who has had to lead her children in spite of the circumstances into their future.

To every father who's had to lead his family through fires of adversity and maintain his role as God's priest in the home.

To every visionary who has led their vision through the appearances of impossibility, out to the other side of achievability.

To every business person who has had to lead their workers through the lean times, as well as the productive.

To every minister of the gospel, who has had to lead other people into the presence of God, in the midst of rejection or false accusation, or crisis.

I salute you.

You have kept the faith, and you are running the race. Henceforth there is laid up for you a crown of righteousness, which the Lord thy God will give you at that day.
(II Timothy 4:7, 8)

1

Great LEADERS Pursue Information, Average LEADERS Propagate Hearsay.

◆ You have no right to anything unpursued.

◆ Your future is contained in your hunger for information.

◆ Information is only as believable as the source, and only as credible as the motive.

Winning Words

When wisdom entereth into thine heart, and knowledge is pleasant unto thy soul; Discretion shall preserve thee, understanding shall keep thee: Proverbs 2:10-11

2

Great LEADERS Build Memorials, Average LEADERS Create Casualties.

1 Leaders are as accountable for the lives of others, as they are for their own.

2 Success is determined by what others are able to do, as a result of something you have done for them.

3 What you release multiplies. What you restrict, dies.

—— L e a d e r ' s   W o r d s ——

And when he looked on him, he was afraid, and said, What is it, Lord? And he said unto him, Thy prayers and thine alms are come up for a memorial before God.   Acts 10:4

3

Great LEADERS Prepare Others For Their Future, Average LEADERS Hold Others In Their Present.

❶ If you can't see someone in the "Palace" you will never take them out of the "Fields."

❷ Your achievements will always link you to teaching others to achieve.

❸ Your legacy will not be determined by what you teach others to do, but by what you release others to do.

--- Leader's Words ---

And the seventy returned again with joy, saying, Lord, even the devils are subject unto us through thy name.
Luke 10:17

4

Great LEADERS Embrace Facts, Average LEADERS Embrace Rumor.

1. Truth makes you accountable.

2. Rumor is never exposed, until it's interrogated.

3. Your response to accusation, determines how far off course your enemy can detour you.

Leader's Words

And ye shall know the truth, and the truth shall make you free. John 8:32

5

Great LEADERS Seek Production, Average LEADERS Seek Position.

1 Titles never supersede ability.

2 Your duration in the "Prison" is determined by your problem-solving for somebody in the "Palace."

3 The wise network, the ignorant compete.

Leader's Words

And Pharaoh said unto Joseph, I have dreamed a dream, and there is none that can interpret it: and I have heard say of thee, that thou canst understand a dream to interpret it. Genesis 41:15

6

Great LEADERS Risk Reputation, Average LEADERS Protect It.

❶ The moment you reach for the "Underdog," you force the reality of false friendships to emerge.

❷ If you never have the reputation of a "Mender," you will never have a reputation worth keeping.

❸ Controversy doesn't surround those in error, as much as it does those trying to change it.

Leader's Words

Brethren, if a man be overtaken in a fault, ye which are spiritual, restore such an one in the spirit of meekness...
Galatians 6:1

7

Great LEADERS Protect Their Focus, Average LEADERS Protect Their Pride.

1 Focus unprotected, is focus unproductive.

2 Pride will keep you in a state of denial, that truth has no access to.

3 Never defend your focus to those not helping you reach your destination.

L e a d e r ' s   W o r d s

A double minded man is unstable in all his ways.
James 1:8

8

Great LEADERS Practice Integrity, Average LEADERS Preach About It.

1 The more that integrity flows through your life, the more unethical people will be uncomfortable around your life.

2 Integrity is "birthed" by the wrong you have caused others, and "sculptured" by the wrong others have caused you.

3 When you have to defend what you do right, it's because people can't see it.

─────── L e a d e r ' s   W o r d s ───────

The just man walketh in his integrity: his children are blessed after him. Proverbs 20:7

8

9

Great LEADERS Show Others Where To Go, Average LEADERS Tell Others Where To Go.

1 Leadership is the desire to teach, control is the desire to dictate.

2 The only mentors that are qualified to teach you, are those who have mastered where you are going.

3 You are either someone's "usher" into their future, or a "detour" from it.

Leader's Words

Be ye followers of me, even as I also am of Christ.
I Corinthians 11:1

10

Great LEADERS Care, Average LEADERS Control.

❶ Confused protegés never seek help from condemning mentors.

❷ The level of help that a protegé reaches for, will be determined by the level of safety they feel when reaching.

❸ People will be touched by how much you care, more than impressed by how much you know.

───── L e a d e r ' s   W o r d s ─────

Thus speaketh the LORD of hosts, saying, Execute true judgment, and show mercy and compassions every man to his brother: Zechariah 7:9

11

Great Leaders Recognize Error, Average LEADERS Justify It.

❶ You must change error, quicker than you recognize it.

❷ The longer you tolerate something, the longer it controls you.

❸ Incompetent results, are the proof of an incapable belief system.

L e a d e r ' s   W o r d s

Who can understand his errors? cleanse thou me from secret faults. Psalms 19:12

12

Great LEADERS Motivate Everyone To Do Something, Average LEADERS Motivate Someone To Do Everything.

1 Championships are never won by a winning player, only a winning team.

2 If people don't know their position, they'll never know their purpose.

3 Your level of delegation, determines your level of victory.

──────── L e a d e r ' s   W o r d s ────────

They which builded on the wall, and they that bare burdens, with those that laded, every one with one of his hands wrought in the work... Nehemiah 4:17

13

Great LEADERS Leave Legacies, Average LEADERS Leave Tragedies.

1 What you build for yourself, will die when you do.

2 What you leave for others, will depend on what you have mastered, or what has mastered you.

3 Success is the proof you have built something that can be multiplied in the next generation.

Leader's Words

When I call to remembrance the unfeigned faith that is in thee, which dwelt first in thy grandmother Lois, and thy mother Eunice; and I am persuaded that in thee also. II Timothy 1:5

14

Great LEADERS Develop Loyalty, Average LEADERS Demand It.

◆ Position does not produce accountability...relationship does.

◆ Those that do not have your heart, will not have your interest.

◆ You will only trust someone you have taught.

L e a d e r ' s   W o r d s

Faithful are the wounds of a friend; but the kisses of an enemy are deceitful. Proverbs 27:6

15

Great LEADERS Are Motivated By Completion, Average LEADERS Are Motivated By Beginning.

❶ Thoughts decide potential. Plans decide direction.

❷ Unrealistic goals produce undesirable memories.

❸ "Conceivers" are never "achievers," until they recruit "completers."

―――――― L e a d e r ' s   W o r d s ――――――

I have glorified thee on the earth: I have finished the work which thou gavest me to do. John 17:4

16

Great LEADERS Defend Their Cause, Average LEADERS Defend Their Calling.

1 If you're worth is not obvious to others, it's not important to others.

2 Never stall your destination on the detour of self-defense.

3 Never defend 16 X 20 potential to 3 X 5 envy.

L e a d e r ' s   W o r d s

Watch ye, stand fast in the faith, quit you like men, be strong. I Corinthians 16:13

17

Great LEADERS Link Themselves With Greatness, Average LEADERS Compare Themselves With Greatness.

1 Those that stop learning, stop leading.

2 The "Portrait of your Destination," is painted by those you are associated with.

3 Proof of the kind of future God has assigned for you, is determined by the kind of mentor He links you to.

───── L e a d e r ' s   W o r d s ─────

And Elijah said unto Elisha, Tarry here, I pray thee; for the LORD hath sent me to Bethel. And Elisha said unto him, As the LORD liveth, and as thy soul liveth, I will not leave thee... II Kings 2:2

18

Great LEADERS Measure Success By Effectiveness, Average LEADERS Measure Success By Numbers.

1 The only way to achieve success, is to define success.

2 The accuracy of your plans, determines the pace to the end result.

3 You will never leave the center of your success, until you leave the center of your expertise.

───── L e a d e r ' s   W o r d s ─────

And my speech and my preaching was not with enticing words of man's wisdom, but in demonstration of the Spirit and of power: I Corinthians 2:4

19

Great LEADERS Do One Thing Excellent, Average LEADERS Do Five Things Mediocre.

1 The difference between "excellence" and "mediocrity," is what you tolerate.

2 Excellent people will conquer, what average people will complain about.

3 Mediocrity disqualifies you from recognition.

Leader's Words

In all things showing thyself a pattern of good works: in doctrine showing uncorruptness, gravity, sincerity,
Titus 2:7

20

Great LEADERS Respond, Average LEADERS React.

1 Somebody somewhere, is always watching how you handle your life.

2 Your reaction determines how much God can defend you, and your enemy can distract you.

3 Emotional reactions will cost you, what informational responses will save you.

─── L e a d e r ' s   W o r d s ───

He that answereth a matter before he heareth it, it is folly and shame unto him. Proverbs 18:13

21
Great LEADERS Ask Questions, Average LEADERS Ask Opinions.

1 Never let pride protect a void that only information can fill.

2 Information begins with interrogation.

3 Questions reveal your willingness to overcome the insecurity of reaching, for the possibility of learning.

Leader's Words

If any of you lack wisdom, let him ask of God, that giveth to all men liberally, and upbraideth not; and it shall be given him. James 1:5

22

Great LEADERS Teach, Average LEADERS Dictate.

1 If someone can't approach you, they can't learn from you.

2 The quality of the investment in another, determines the quality of the return in you.

3 The difference between teachers and dictators, is there comfortability with questions.

Leader's Words

And when he had called all the people unto him, he said unto them, Hearken unto me every one of you, and understand: Mark 7:14

23

Great LEADERS Are Motivated By Another's Achievements, Average LEADERS Are Intimidated By Them.

1 Never envy another's success, more than you study it.

2 The wise think they are a continuation of the "legacy." The ignorant think they are the founders of the "dynasty."

3 Those who study champions, become champions.

――――― L e a d e r ' s   W o r d s ―――――

There shall not any man be able to stand before thee all the days of thy life: as I was with Moses, so I will be with thee: I will not fail thee, nor forsake thee.
Joshua 1:5

24

Great LEADERS Look For The "Long Haul," Average LEADERS Look For The "Quick Fix."

❶ Longevity gives you an opinion.

❷ Nothing significant will ever be without the price of time.

❸ If you're married to your destination, temporary seasons won't frustrate you.

——— L e a d e r ' s   W o r d s ———

Seest thou a man diligent in his business? he shall stand before kings; he shall not stand before mean men.
Proverbs 22:29

25

Great LEADERS Are Married To A Result, Average LEADERS Are Married To A Method.

◆ Plans require pruning, in order to keep producing.

◆ You will never discover the pleasures of "winning," until you discover the "principles of order."

◆ God cannot influence a plan you do not have.

L e a d e r ' s   W o r d s

Prove all things; hold fast that which is good.
I Thessalonians 5:21

26

Great LEADERS Use Pain To Get Better, Average LEADERS Use Pain To Get Bitter.

1 Pain will never promote change, as long as it protects resentment.

2 God will use the "platform of pain" when He is unable to use the "access door of pleasure."

3 Anything you can't release, you can't rebuild.

Leader's Words

He healeth the broken in heart, and bindeth up their wounds. Psalms 147:3

27

Great LEADERS See Time As An Ally, Average LEADERS See Time As An Obstacle.

1 God will keep you in your present season long enough to become over qualified for it.

2 When something comes into your life, it is a prophecy of something that is leaving it.

3 God will use time to birth the conviction of patience in you, so your enemy will be unable to use the weapon of impatience against you, to sabotage your destiny.

Leader's Words

To every thing there is a season, and a time to every purpose under the heaven: Ecclesiastes 3:1

28

Great LEADERS Learn From Their Past, Average LEADERS Live In It.

1 The only way you will rewrite your past is if you rewrite your present.

2 When you rehearse past mistakes, you prepare yourself to repeat them.

3 Spend more time preparing for your next victory, than you do looking back at your last one.

─── Leader's Words ───

Brethren, I count not myself to have apprehended: but this one thing I do, forgetting those things which are behind, and reaching forth unto those things which are before, Philippians 3:13

29

Great LEADERS Assess Their Weaknesses, Average LEADERS Cover Them.

1 Weaknesses are just undeveloped strengths.

2 Never be transparent about your weakness, to those incapable of strengthening them.

3 Never put yourself in a position where a weakness is forced to defend you.

Leader's Words

To another faith by the same Spirit; to another the gifts of healing by the same Spirit; I Corinthians 12:9

30

Great LEADERS Have Purposeful Relationships, Average LEADERS Have Political Ones.

1 Never allow those walking outside of their assignment, to wander into yours.

2 If somebody doesn't change by being in your life, that's proof they did not come into your life to change.

3 Ethical people link with other ethical people because "iron sharpens iron." Unethical people link with other unethical people because there is no threat by truth to expose error.

── L e a d e r ' s   W o r d s ──

Blessed is the man that walketh not in the counsel of the ungodly, nor standeth in the way of sinners, nor sitteth in the seat of the scornful. Psalms 1:1

31

Great LEADERS Finish, Average LEADERS Watch.

1 Your focus will always determine your proximity to the finish line.

2 You can't change your life until you can change your routine.

3 Champions go to the top, with or without the approval of others.

L e a d e r ' s   W o r d s

I have fought a good fight, I have finished my course, I have kept the faith: II Timothy 4:7

Signs & Wonders Partners

•••

I want ot take this time and personally say how *"Excited"* and *"Grateful"* I am to God for the many friends from all parts of these United States that have become linked to this *Ministry of the Holy Spirit* with their prayers and with their monthly seed into this fertile soil of this harvest field. Having the privilege of the taking the message of this *"Wonderful Companion"* to thousands around the country in both live crusades and media outreach, has been a joy that words cannot express.

I know there are still yet many of you that *God's voice* is going to speak to, to become connected with this ministry as a special *"Signs and Wonders Partner"* both prayerfully and financially to help take this message of knowing the *Holy Spirit* to so many that still need to hear it.

Would you ask the *Holy Spirit* today about becoming linked with me at *$10.00 each month*, or whatever *He* lays upon your heart so we can reach this critical objective together. Remember, *whenever you react to His voice, He reacts to your future*.

I'll look forward to hearing from you.

☐ **Yes, J. Konrad I want to link myself to you with my monthly seed of $_____ a month for the spreading of this needed message around the world!**

Name _____

Address _____

City _____ State _____ Zip _____

Phone (___) _____

Clip & Mail To: Spirit & Life Ministries
P.O. BOX 41010   MINNEAPOLIS, MN 55441

Clip & Mail

Let Me Agree With You In Prayer For Your Need!

Y̶ou are daily upon my heart and your needs matter greatly to me. Don't ever think that you are alone. I want to agree with you that the Holy Spirit will bring the provision of God in your life!

_____

_____

_____

_____

_____

_____

_____

_____

_____

_____

_____

_____

_____

Name _____

Address _____

City _____ State _____ Zip _____

Phone ( )_____

Clip & Mail To: Spirit & Life Ministries
P.O. BOX 41010   MINNEAPOLIS, MN 55441

Clip & Mail

More Power-Packed Teaching
From J. Konrad Hölè

The Leading Of His Spirit

Join J. Konrad for this "Explosive" and "In-Depth" study on how the Holy Spirit leads you more by "Purpose, Principals and Protocal" than He does by Euphoria, Emotion, and Excitement. The greatest seasons of your life are just ahead, LED BY HIS SPIRIT.

$20.00 (4 tape series)

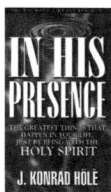

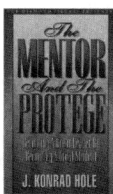

In His Presence

Find out the life changing secrets of Kind David's revelation of how to live in the Presence of God. The most incredible breakthroughs in your life are about to take place just be being in His Presence.

$15.00 (3 tape series)

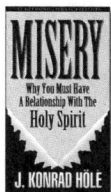

Diary Of The Holy Spirit

Discover the benefits of how to Commune, Flow, Discern, and Listen to the Holy Spirit who Jesus said would be with you Always. Your greatest relationship is one revelation away.

$15.00 (3 tape series)

Misery

Discover David's revelation principles from Psalms 16:11, that the only true place of joy was in God's presence, and that anything outside His presence was not designed to satisfy you, but rather would be a source of "Misery."

$20.00 (4 tape series)

The Mentor And The Protege

What is a *Mentor*? A gift by *God* to insure the success of completing your *Assignment*. What is a *Protege*? A person whose future depends on the impartation from somebody who has already been where they are going. In this impactive teaching you will understand the purpose of mentoring.

$20.00 (4 tape series)

"The Diamond Library For Achievers"
Several Dynamic Topics:

Build Your Complete Achiever Library!

Obedience

Join J. Konrad for this "Impactive" study on the "Power" of OBEDIENCE and its ability to be the bridge from "Where You Are," to "Where You Want To Be ," and God's ability to react to your life everytime you follow one of "His Instructions."
$10.00 (2 tapes)

Time

Join J. Konrad for this "Impactive" study on the "Currency of TIME," its ability to form your "Destiny" around you, and its critical role in developing your relationship with the Holy Spirit.
$10.00 (2 tapes)

Focus

Join J. Konrad for this "Impactive" study on the Force of "FOCUS," and its ability to enable you to walk through the "Valleys of Distraction," and complete your life assignment!
$10.00 (2 tapes)

Send Your Order In Today!

Seed-Faith

Join J. Konrad for this "Impactive" study on the "Power Of Seed Movement" in your life, and your ability to take something God has placed in your hand, to create something God has ordained in your life.
$10.00 (2 tapes)

Warfare

Join J. Konrad for this "Impactive" study of how you were not called to be a "Captive," you were called to be a "Deliverer."
$10.00 (2 tapes)

Direction

Join J. Konrad for this "Impactive" study on how the "HOLY SPIRIT" answers one of the most pivotal questions ever in your life... the question of DIRECTION.!
$10.00 (2 tapes)

Don't let these opportunities pass you by! Rush your order in today. Fill out the form below. Please print clearly and legibly. Ask the Holy Spirit what Seed He would have you to sow into this world-changing ministry.

Title	Qty.	Price	Total
The Leading Of His Spirit (Tapes)		$	$
In His Presence (Tapes)		$	$
The Diary Of The Holy Spirit (Tapes)		$	$
Misery (Tapes)		$	$
The Mentor And The Protege (Tapes)		$	$
Library For Achievers - Time (Tapes)		$	$
Library For Achievers - Obedience (Tapes)		$	$
Library For Achievers - Focus (Tapes)		$	$
Library For Achievers - Seed-Faith (Tapes)		$	$
Library For Achievers - Warfare (Tapes)		$	$
Library For Achievers - Direction (Tapes)		$	$
1 Item......................$2 - S/H	Shipping/Handling		$
2 Items...................$3 - S/H	Seed-Faith Gift		$
3 or more Items.....$4 - S/H	Total		$

☐ J. Konrad, please send me my **FREE** copy of your *Spirit & Life Talk* newsletter.

☐ Check   ☐ Money Order   ☐ Visa   ☐ MasterCard

Card No. ☐☐☐☐☐☐☐☐☐☐☐☐☐☐☐☐

Exp. Date _____ Signature _____

Name _____

Address _____

City _____ State _____ Zip _____

Phone (_____) _____

Clip & Mail To: Spirit & Life Ministries
P.O. BOX 41010   MINNEAPOLIS, MN 55441

Clip & Mail

Choose From These Exciting Titles! Books that will bring a Breakthrough... Your life will be challenged and changed with revelation knowledge!

Diamonds For Daily Living

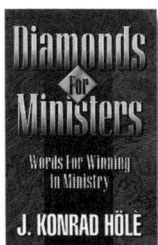

Diamonds For Ministers

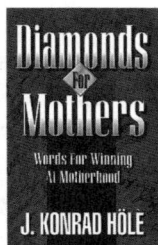

Diamonds For Mothers

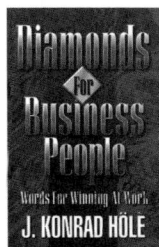

Diamonds For Business People

You Were Born A Champion... Don't Die A Loser!

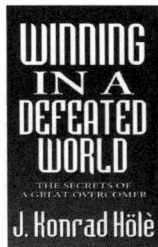

Winning In A Defeated World

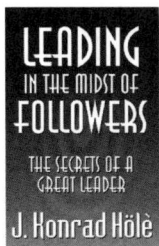

Leading In the Midst Of Followers

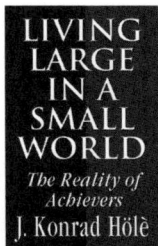

Living Large In A Small World

See the next page for details on how to order your personal copies of these books!

"Literature Evangelism Team"

Order Form

☐ Yes, J. Konrad, I want to be a part of this "Evangelism Breakthrough" so that I may affect those that God links me to with the power of revelation knowledge.

Order a set of 10 copies of any title for $10. You may also mix titles of the books to bring a total of 10 copies for $10. Order for your friends and family!

Title	Qty. (Sets of 10)	Price	Total
Diamonds For Daily Living		x $10	$
Diamonds For Ministers		x $10	$
Diamonds For Mothers		x $10	$
Diamonds For Business People		x $10	$
You Were Born A Champion...		x $10	$
Winning In A Defeated World		x $10	$
Leading In The Midst Of Followers		x $10	$
Living Large In A Small World		x $10	$
		Shipping	$
Add $2 For Shipping		Seed-Faith Gift	$
		Total	$

☐ Check   ☐ Money Order   ☐ Visa   ☐ MasterCard

Card No. [ ][ ][ ][ ][ ][ ][ ][ ][ ][ ][ ][ ][ ][ ][ ][ ][ ][ ]

Exp. Date _____ Signature _____

Name _____

Address _____

City _____ State _____ Zip _____

Phone (___) _____

Clip & Mail To: Spirit & Life Ministries
P.O. BOX 41010   MINNEAPOLIS, MN 55441

Clip & Mail